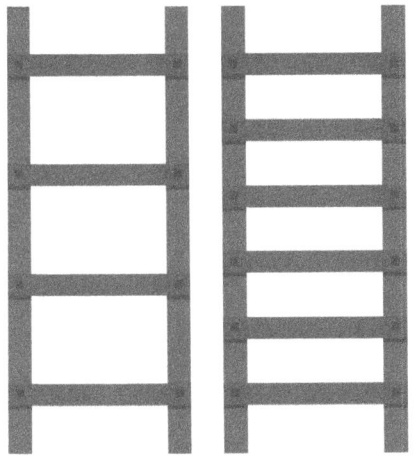

SARA LOUISE MUHR

How to fight everyday discrimination

A guide to inclusive DEI behaviors at work

Copyright ©2024 Sara Louise Muhr

All rights reserved. No part of this publication may be reproduced, stored in any retrieval system or transmitted in any form or by any means: electronic, mechanical, photocopying, recording or otherwise without the prior permission of the publishers.

Translated from Danish by Amalie Lind Ditlevsen and further edited and adjusted to an international context by the author. The original version is entitled 'Hvordan bekæmper vi hverdagsdiskrimination?' and published by Informations Forlag.

Sara Louise Muhr is Professor of Diversity & Leadership at the Department of Business Humanities and Law at Copenhagen Business School in Denmark. Professor Muhr can be reached via email: slm.bhl@cbs.dk.

Book consultant: Malene Bendtsen (Publishing Rebel)

Book cover & interior design: Bookcoverhub.com

ISBN: 9798334894013

TABLE OF CONTENTS

Preface 5

The challenge: Invisible discrimination 17

    Everyday discrimination and legislation 18
    What does everyday
    discrimination typically look like? 21
    Common characteristics
     of everyday discrimination 44
    Consequences of everyday discrimination 53

Status: Policies and minority focus 59

    Zero tolerance 60
    Voluntariness 62
    Minority initiatives 65
    Bias training 66

Change: You, me, and all of us 69

    Knowledge, attitude, and behavior........................ 69
    From the individual
    to the collective and the collegial 71
    It is—and *should* be—difficult 73
    Everyday inclusion 76

Final thoughts.. 87

References 93

Endnotes.. 95

Preface

Whenever leaders who are seeking to understand and fight discrimination within their organizations approach me, they emphasize the same thing: Each and every one of them has a completely unique organizational culture and/or history, which makes their particular situation special. They are not strictly wrong. All organizations are different; they are shaped by the various professions that they are composed of, their organizational histories, the people working in them, and many other similar factors. However, when it comes to discrimination, research very clearly indicates common features across professions, industries, and organizational cultures. Thus, when seeking to address the problem of discrimination, leaders would do well to realize that their respective organizations are probably not very unique in this regard, for better or for worse.

Discrimination is defined as unequal treatment based on identity markers, such as gender, race, and sexual orientation. Discrimination can be found in the structure of our society, including the processes of our workplaces; these include the ways in which new employees are recruited and promotions are given, in addition to various everyday interactions, such as meetings, lunch breaks, and small talk in the hallways or at the coffee machine. It emerges from our—typically unconscious—assumptions about other people's identities, and it is deeply rooted in historical and cultural perceptions of difference, which usually operate within various binary hierarchies: male/female, white/non-white, and heterosexual/homosexual. These binaries manifest as sexism, racism, and heterosexism, respectively. Hence, these "-isms" are ideology-based assumptions about identity, and discrimination is the inappropriate actions that result from such assumptions.

In this book, I focus on everyday discrimination. As the term indicates, everyday discrimination refers to discrimination embedded in everyday interactions. While more direct and overt cases of discrimination occasionally make the headlines, everyday discrimination is difficult to detect and address. This, however, does not mean that it is any less damaging for individuals or organizations. When individuals do not thrive at work, their performance drops, and after a while, they may even leave the organization. Learning to identify and fight everyday discrimination at work is important, not only for the personal well-being of employees but also for organizational performance. This is why the features and impact of everyday discrimination are key to working actively with diversity, equity, and inclusion (DEI). Diversity is the composition of different people in a team or an organization. Working with diversity through the lens of equity means working for equal opportunities despite people's differences. Finally, inclusion is a measure of whether a unique individual feels a sense of belonging in a group.[1]

For more than twenty years, I have been researching everyday discrimination in the workplace as well as its underlying social ideologies, such as sexism, racism, and heterosexism. For the last ten of these years, I have been working actively with leaders and organizations that wish to fight everyday discrimination and increase employee well-being. Based on my theoretical and practical experience, I argue that there are multiple common features in the way everyday discrimination manifests and is expressed across different workplaces and in the way employees are adversely affected by it. Similarly, I see the same dire consequences for organizational performance and competitive advantage across different types of organizations and industries. Consequently, it is also possible to define a wide range of common inclusive behaviors that can be mobilized in the fight against everyday discrimination in different organizational settings. This is what this book is about: identifying and fighting everyday discrimination. Let me set the scene for this task with a few examples from some organizations—each one notably different from the others—I have worked with in recent years.[2]

We begin with a large Danish organization in the construction industry. Mehmet is a newly hired apprentice. He has already developed good relationships with his colleagues on the team. One colleague in particular has been looking after him and making sure that he is introduced to all the various aspects of the job. Their interactions are friendly and informal. After his first week, Mehmet has to clock his hours on his time card. The more experienced colleague offers to take care of it for him, and for this, he asks Mehmet for his full name. On hearing the name, the colleague laughs and says, "Wow, that is a real terrorist name." Later in the day, the colleague asks Mehmet if he likes football, and Mehmet answers that he is a big fan of Brøndby IF (a Danish team). The colleague instantly replies, "That is such a Paki club." These comments make Mehmet very uncomfortable, but he is also concerned about speaking up, as it may have negative consequences for him.

The second example takes us to the Danish headquarters of a large international consulting firm. Julie is twenty-seven years old and has worked for the organization for a year and a half. She loves her job and working long hours, and she is thriving in the competitive environment of the consulting business. One day, her manager approaches her and says, "Julie, I think you are working too much. I think you should go home earlier. We would very much like to keep you when you eventually start a family, so it would be great if you would learn to take care of yourself and go home a bit earlier." At first, Julie is touched by his concern, but after giving it some thought, she finds this to be a rather weird thing to say. He has never said anything like that to any of her male colleagues, whose work habits are the exact same as hers, and he never leaves early himself. Moreover, everyone in the organization knows that no one has ever been promoted for going home early. Julie is ambitious, and she does not even know yet whether she wants children or, if so, when. It is also not something she has ever talked about in the workplace. Why is her manager advising her, but not her male colleagues, to work less? She cannot really pinpoint why, but she gets a sense of being talked down to.

The third example takes us to a Danish university. Peter is teaching a new class of students, and he has been looking forward to getting to know them. As he is developing a relationship with the class, one student, Emilie, starts paying him an unusual amount of attention. Peter notices how Emilie stands very close to him whenever he is talking to a group of students after class. Over time, Emilie's attention intensifies, and she also starts attending his other classes. One day, as Peter is reading one of her papers and checking the references, he finds that one of them contains a direct link to a pornographic website. He is shocked. He decides to confront Emilie and tell her to stop, but Emilie does not understand why he does not like the attention. Her behavior continues. Peter tells his colleagues about the situation, but they laugh at him. He then decides to confer with his head of department, who also laughs at him and says, "It is funny seeing the university's biggest man being so scared of such a little girl." To some extent, Peter agrees. He realizes that the situation is rather untraditional and that he is not actually scared. He cannot exactly explain why, but he finds the situation uncomfortable. Maybe he is more bothered by his colleagues' responses than by her actions?[3]

For the fourth and final example, we turn to a Danish public organization. Martin is making his way to the reception to meet a candidate whom he is interviewing for a new position. He has a very good feeling about her, and he is looking forward to meeting her and finding out if she is the right candidate for the job. He greets her by politely shaking her hand and welcoming her, and then they walk toward the meeting room, where the interview will take place. They engage in small talk on the way. Martin asks her what her husband does for a living, to which she replies that she does not have a husband but a wife. Martin becomes a bit dumbfounded. It is not that he does not accept homosexuality; he was just not expecting that answer. After the interview, he is annoyed by the way he framed the question and by his own reaction. He should have known better and not made such assumptions based on her appearance. The mood definitely shifted after that particular question. He still cannot explain why, but he felt a bit awkward, and she clearly did not like the situation either. Their previously good chemistry changed, and he cannot figure out whether it is affecting his assessment of her.

All four examples are different, occurring in different types of organizations and involving different people and situations. They do, however, share the trait that they are all examples of everyday discrimination emerging from stereotypical assumptions about other people's personalities, lives, choices, and preferences. Stereotypical assumptions result from the aforementioned "-isms." Sexism is the ideology that produces the norms for what is considered "normal" and "natural" behavior, attire, choice of study, family, and career, among other factors, based on your assumed gender. Racism is the ideology that results from perceived links between physical characteristics (such as skin color, facial features, and hair texture) and personality traits. In the racist ideology, some bodies appear "neutral," whereas other bodies are racialized; that is, "race"[4] is socially ascribed to some individuals, associating them with certain values and customs. Racism is often reinforced by Islamophobia (or Christonormativity), in which religious practices are linked to certain racialized features. Heterosexism is the assumption that all individuals are heterosexual—or the conviction that heterosexuality is the "normal" and "natural" orientation.

Stereotypical assumptions are a result of the way the aforementioned "-isms" are internalized by individuals. We are not necessarily aware of these assumptions, as they are ingrained opinions about what can be regarded as "normal" and "natural." Even if we consciously reject stereotypes, a lot of our knowledge, language, and traditions are based on them. If you are not completely convinced by this, consider how many people in the so-called Western[5] world tend to picture a man when thinking of a police officer or the CEO of a big company or how many view not eating pork as strange, all while believing it is the most "normal" thing to celebrate Christmas. We may be surprised (maybe even impressed?) if the CEO of a large Nordic company is dark-skinned. When walking the streets of cities such as Copenhagen, London, and Berlin, we may look twice (maybe even think it is "too much"?) if we see two men kissing in public, but we barely even notice the many heterosexual couples doing the same. These reactions are the results of the assumptions that are unconsciously embedded in all of us, and they influence our opinions about the people we meet.

Within the first few seconds of meeting a new person, we inadvertently assess them based on their physical features. Our brains use unconscious assumptions to quickly and effectively decode who the new person is, what competencies they may have, and what set of values they may live by. In other words, we do not even have time to actively think before our brains have already assessed the person standing in front of us. In the field of DEI, this cognitive mechanism is known as bias.

Everyday discrimination stems from stereotypical assumptions that are activated automatically and often unconsciously in our social interactions, and it materializes in humorous remarks, small talk, or casually stated opinions that are rarely meant to be offensive. Furthermore, everyday discrimination is typically not illegal (although the boundaries are often vague, as explained below), and it can be difficult to detect. Or rather, you feel it when everyday discrimination stems from stereotypes about your own identity, but you are rarely aware of how the manifestations of your own basic assumptions may discriminate against others. In fact, people will typically deny any discriminatory intent when confronted about it. Everyday discrimination is often excused as a joke or "part of the jargon," as in Mehmet's example, or it could be disguised as care, as in Julie's case. Sometimes, discrimination is not taken seriously, as in Peter's story, or it can be based on normative assumptions about other people's private lives, as in Martin's case. Thus, it is difficult to spot, and most people—until they take a more thorough look, that is—do not even believe that it exists in their organizations. However, everyday discrimination is highly likely to be found in all organizations, across all industries, and at all levels. Even in organizations that are committed to working with progressive business models or are professionally engaged with DEI, we find everyday discrimination. Actually, it can be even more difficult for these organizations to see it happening within their ranks because they are convinced that they are already engaged in "goodness" or "critical reasoning."

As everyday discrimination is so difficult to identify, its extent and consequences can be equally difficult—or even more difficult—to address and fight. In this book, I explain what everyday discrimination is, detailing how it affects individuals, organizations, and societies. This book shows you how to detect everyday discrimination in your own everyday life; it also helps you understand its implications and supplies you with the tools needed to begin the fight against everyday discrimination, no matter the organization you work in or the level you work at. We may not be able to end everyday discrimination completely, as the stereotypes it stems from are so deeply and unconsciously entrenched in all of us and are so prominent when we make quick decisions. However, we can all become better at changing our behavior and incorporating new routines and habits that minimize discrimination and mitigate its damaging effects.

The challenge: Invisible discrimination

The challenge: Invisible discrimination

Discrimination is unequal treatment based on identity markers, such as gender, race, and sexual orientation. Discrimination is problematic on several levels. At the societal level, discrimination creates unequal access to certain professions as well as promotions, in addition to resulting in unequal pay. At the individual level, experiencing discrimination can lead to frustration, stress, and even depression or anxiety. At the organizational level, discrimination is problematic because of two aspects: First, it creates homogeneous teams (due to the aforementioned unequal access), but teams need diverse perspectives to make solid and well-informed decisions. Second, individuals who are the object of everyday discrimination (due to their minority status) often feel less included and, hence, do not perform as well as individuals from the majority.

Everyday discrimination is the most challenging form of discrimination due to its insidiousness. It operates latently, causing inequality, distress, and lower performance without us even realizing it.

Everyday discrimination and legislation

The fact that everyday discrimination can be difficult to identify also makes it difficult to fight via legislation. Nevertheless, it is best to begin with the legal perspective, using it to understand how everyday discrimination differs from other types of discrimination. In principle, Danish[6] legislation protects individuals from discrimination. The Danish Discrimination Act[7] contains, for instance, injunctions against discrimination based on "race, skin color, religious beliefs, political views, sexual orientation, age, disability and national, social or ethnic origin." The Danish Act on Equal Treatment[8] focuses on gender and contains injunctions against discrimination based on gender. These legal texts cover all aspects of employment, from job applications to workplace conditions and even a potential termination.

The Danish Discrimination Act and the Danish Act on Equal Treatment apply not only to formal employment relations but also to general workplace conditions (i.e., everyday scenarios, such as a manager remaining passive while an employee is being discriminated against).[9] According to the legislation, it is the employer's responsibility to ensure that discrimination does not occur in the workplace, just like it is the employer's responsibility to make sure that there is a good physical and psychosocial work environment in the organization. However, this can be rather difficult, as it raises the question of what is considered a good work environment and to whom this applies. Even within more formal processes, such as recruitment and termination, it can be difficult to guard against discrimination. However, these processes tend to be planned and carefully considered, and here, discrimination is typically confined to one particular situation or instance that, hopefully, stands out as an anomaly. Formal processes can (or should) at least be professionalized to ensure that stereotypes are addressed and that biases are blocked, thereby minimizing discrimination.

However, when considering how to avoid discrimination in everyday workplace situations and how to provide a good psychosocial work environment, the matter becomes more complex.

Discrimination does not occur only in formal contexts, such as job interviews, meetings, and seminars. It also happens in informal contexts, such as at the coffee machine, in the canteen, and at company parties or team-building events. Furthermore, people have different boundaries, which may even change on a daily basis and depend on the context. This makes everyday discrimination extremely challenging to tackle in professional contexts. However, despite its subtlety, I argue in this book that it *is* possible to improve our ability to identify discrimination as well as our understanding of how it manifests within organizations and how it is perceived subjectively by individual employees.

Everyday discrimination is closely related to more explicit and overt types of discrimination, making it difficult to differentiate between explicit and implicit types of discrimination and to determine exactly what is legal and illegal. As the two are entangled, it can be helpful to visualize discrimination as a spiral that begins with everyday discrimination, evolves into explicit and hostile discrimination, and ultimately leads to assaults and hate crimes. This process is reinforced in a circular manner because everyday discrimination—which may seem innocent and banal in isolated cases—is normalized through repetition, which legitimizes more direct and abusive types of discrimination, leading to assaults and hate crimes. Simultaneously, the occurrence of hostile discrimination and hate crimes often ends up trivializing everyday discrimination and pushing the boundaries of what is considered acceptable behavior that we should simply "put up with." For instance, when particularly abusive discrimination occurs in "other" parts of society (or the world), it will often be used as a justification for why we should be content with how we are living in "our" part of society (or the world), where discrimination is more subtle. Discrimination experienced by individuals in Nordic workplaces, for example, is often trivialized when compared to "worse" cases in other parts of the world. Similarly, discrimination experienced in some sectors or professions may be downplayed by comparing it with how "bad" others are.

What does everyday discrimination typically look like?

Discrimination is, as stated above, unequal treatment based on identity markers, such as gender, race, and sexual orientation. In the book *Leading Through Bias*, which I co-authored with Poornima Luthra in 2023, we divide a person's identity into fifteen dimensions to detail what discrimination may look like in the workplace. These are gender; sexual orientation; age; physical abilities and health; appearances and race; education; experience and skills; personality; neurodiversity; mental health; culture, ethnicity, and nationality; beliefs and practices; marital and parenthood choices; location and geography; and socioeconomic background.

More dimensions can certainly be added. In the following sections, and in line with the short format of this book, I focus on the dimensions that have been researched most thoroughly: gender, race, and sexual orientation. This does not mean that these are the most important dimensions or the ones that lead to the most severe or pervasive forms of everyday discrimination. To emphasize this, I follow up this discussion with an examination of the intersectionality of these dimensions (i.e., the way in which they are connected and always influenced by other identity markers). All identity dimensions and intersections are unique, but people's experiences of discrimination on the basis of these share some common traits. Thus, I hope that, by focusing on these three dimensions and their intersections, I can show how discrimination occurs on the basis of stereotypical assumptions. While the expressions and experiences of these assumptions are unique, we can identify and fight them in the same ways, regardless of whether they are based on gender, race, sexual orientation, a mix of all three, or something completely different.

Discrimination based on gender

Gender[10] is by far the most researched dimension. This is because (binary) gender is the only dimension that can be consistently compared across various geographical contexts, as it is legal to both register and measure in many contexts. This is not the case with other dimensions. For instance, an American employer is allowed to ask about and register ethnic background, but it is unthinkable that the same person would ask the applicant their age. In Denmark, it is completely unthinkable that an employer would register the employees' ethnic backgrounds (this is, in fact, illegal), whereas age is something most people explicitly state on their CVs. What is considered legal and/or culturally acceptable to register and measure in one context cannot necessarily be directly translated into another context—except for gender. Therefore, gender is one of the only dimensions that we can meaningfully compare across contexts—and it is a dimension that leads to discrimination in most contexts.

With regard to discrimination based on gender, over the years and across many different national contexts, research has established that we (independent of context) tend to assess men's competencies higher than women's. Several studies have proven this using many different methodologies, of which the so-called CV studies are but one important group. In these studies, CVs are sent out to a large number of people. The CVs are completely identical, with one exception: One half of the recipients get a CV with a male-sounding name on it, while the other half receive a CV with a female-sounding name. The results of these studies are consistent across both geographical and professional contexts. If we believe that the applicant is a man, we tend to evaluate his competencies higher and offer him a higher starting salary; furthermore, we are more likely to offer to mentor him because we estimate his potential to be greater. The last of these points is worth elaborating a bit further, as it shows that changing the focus from competencies to potential will not, contrary to what people often think, result in the recruitment/promotion of more women. Our assessment of potential is as—or more—affected by bias as our assessment of competencies. In somewhat provocative words, it can be said that, when we talk about a person's potential (or talent), we do not know what we are talking about. If we want to be more precise, as well as fair, in our assessment of a person, we have to be very specific with regard to what potential consists of and what competencies a person must possess to be considered talented. A good rule of thumb when considering whether a person has potential is to ask what this potential consists of and why. This forces us to be more precise and helps us minimize the effect of gender bias on our perceptions of potential and talent.

When I say "we," I mean it. This type of discrimination based on gender is not something that only men do to women. Our gendered interpretations of competence and skills are so internalized that everyone is likely to have gender biases. While research consistently shows that gender discrimination primarily affects women, there is equally consistent evidence that women are just as discriminatory toward women as men are.

Furthermore, research shows that we tend to write shorter and less complimentary recommendations for women than for men and that we tend to talk more about women's personalities and appearances but more about men's professional skills when, for instance, giving references. This may seem like an insignificant point, but consider how many jobs are filled through people's informal networks or how much management and HR departments use references from previous business partners/collaborators when recruiting new employees or promoting internally. This tendency is particularly pronounced at the top of the corporate hierarchy. For instance, only approximately 6% of board members in Denmark are hired through open job adverts; the rest are hired through personal networks or by headhunters/recruitment firms (that is, their networks). We should also consider how much people gossip within an organization (and everywhere else) and how much of this gossip is about a people's personality, looks, gender, private life, or other identity markers. How we talk about each other means something.

Regarding personality and how it is often (unconsciously) perceived through the lens of gender, studies show that male leaders are considered more likable compared to female leaders. This type of study goes all the way back to Peter Glick and Susan Fiske's famous American study from 1996, in which they assessed how a large group of people were evaluated with regard to "warmth," meaning how nice they were considered to be as persons, and "competence," meaning how good they were considered to be at their jobs. In 2002, Tomas Eckes built on Glick and Fiske's study and focused specifically on gender in the context of Germany; he found that the more competent women were perceived to be, the lower they scored on likeability. In other words, women's perceived likeability and competency were inversely correlated—the more competent a woman, the less likable she was. The same did not happen with men. Men could more easily be seen as both competent and nice at the same time. To transfer this to an everyday corporate context, it is common to hear assertive female leaders be referred to as "ice queens," "tough," "bossy," "too much," "mini-men," "more man than the men themselves," or even "bitchy," whereas the same assertive behavior from male leaders is often considered "strong," "brave," "impressive," and "to the benefit of the organization." At the same time, female leaders are constantly criticized for neglecting their families, being called names like "raven mothers" (the direct English translation of a Danish derogatory term for a mother who does not take care of her children) or "career women." The term "raven father" does not exist in Danish, nor is "career man" used in any language that I know of. Our language—and thus what we have words for—reveals what we consider "normal" and "natural" and indicates what is outside the norm. With this in mind, we see a tendency for working women to encounter an increasingly narrow set of socially accepted behaviors the higher they climb the organizational ladder. If they are strong and assertive, they are "a bit of a bitch;" if they are gentle and caring, they are not considered to have leadership potential and will not be regarded as "talents." In her work, Joan C. Williams describes this as the tightrope bias (e.g., Williams, 2021), and in my 2019 book *Gendered Leadership* (only available in Danish under the title *Ledelse af Køn*), I illustrate this bias very clearly through interviews with Danish C-suite.

Furthermore, our gendered norms and corresponding expectations regarding the "normal" or "preferred" work-life balance of a person affect men and women differently. This is particularly noticeable in the pervasive expectation that a female employee in her late twenties is headed toward a period of time with parental leave and care responsibilities—an expectation that does not affect men's careers in the same way, even though almost as many men as women become parents! The consequences of this stereotype can be detected in employment statistics, which show that mothers are less likely than women without children to be hired when applying for jobs, whereas fathers are better off as job applicants compared to men who do not have children. We also find these consequences in wage gap statistics, in which women's wages decrease significantly when they have their first child, while men's wages actually increase slightly during the same life phase.

Finally, it is important to emphasize that women are not the only ones impacted by gender discrimination and sexism. Everyone is affected by our stereotypical assumptions about what is considered "normal" or even just "acceptable" for different genders and by our often binary understanding of gender, which separates men from women and leaves no room "in between." Even though fathers appear to be slightly better positioned than men who do not have children (and much better positioned than women with or without children), research still shows that men also have to balance their life choices in relation to their careers. In *Gendered Leadership*, I illustrate how there may be a wider span for socially accepted behavior among male leaders compared to female leaders. Nevertheless, both my research in the Danish context and international studies show that men are also penalized for moving "too far" toward behaviors that are considered "feminine." That is, men may benefit from having children or taking on care responsibilities because people tend to think that it makes them a bit more "human" and are impressed by their "soft skills." However, gender stereotypes also mean that many people will dismiss the idea that fatherhood or care responsibilities could affect men's work in the same way that it is assumed motherhood affects the work and careers of women. Similarly, both international and Danish studies show that, if men request more flexible conditions—such as reduced work hours or a long paternity leave (more than three months in the Danish context)—or prioritize family and emotional life over work in any other way, they are punished more harshly than women. Moreover, research shows that men are often bullied—maybe just "for the fun of it"—if they deviate from stereotypical masculine gender norms by, for instance, choosing more care-focused professions or choosing to be a stay-at-home dad (yet another word that does not seem to exist in Danish and several other languages, although it does appear in English).

In sum, we are influenced by a set of strong socially constructed gender norms that create a very fixed framework for what is considered "normal" and "natural" in relation to our choices regarding our work lives and private lives. Everyday discrimination, specifically everyday sexism in this case, occurs when these gender norms affect what people say to each other and how they interact, ultimately influencing their behaviors and decisions.

Discrimination based on race and ethnicity

In today's society, it may no longer be considered controversial to discuss gender diversity, gender discrimination, or even sexism in our workplaces. In fact, not discussing it and not actively encouraging gender parity can limit an organization's ability to attract new employees. However, it is very different when it comes to race and ethnicity. This is a topic that causes unease in most organizations, particularly in the Nordic context. If we think that discussions about gender are too emotional, they are nothing compared to the emotions involved in discussions about race and ethnicity. In contrast to countries such as the US, England, the Netherlands, and France, racial inequality is traditionally not measured or monitored in the Danish (or Nordic) context. Consequently, people in the Nordic countries often lack broadly accepted terminology to talk about race and racism in a respectful and constructive manner. This is what makes the conversation about racial discrimination profoundly conflicted and unpleasant for many people. As a result, in the Nordic context, racism has been mostly ignored and even denied, often dismissed as a secondary topic in—or even a misunderstanding of—the debate about refugees and immigrants. However, issues of racialization cannot be confined solely to refugees and immigrants, neither in the context of the Nordic labor market nor anywhere else. Research shows that we in the Nordic countries have both a racist labor market and a racist society. This essentially refers to a labor market and a society that are not characterized by equity and thus does not offer equal opportunities to everyone.

Before turning to statistics, let us start by establishing a few terms. As mentioned above, only one human race exists, but the term "race" is used to describe racialized effects—that is, the way different bodies are associated with different attributes.

Consequently, the term "race" does not imply the existence of multiple human races; rather, it refers to how differences in skin color, facial features, hair texture, and eye shape and color influence how people are perceived. This is why researchers prefer to talk about racialization, the process through which bodies are coded, rather than race, understood as a fixed concept.

"Ethnicity" is a term that was originally coined to capture elements such as culture and background, but if we cut to the core, it is most often used to categorize people based on racialized features, such as skin color, as discussed above. After all, what is the difference between someone considered an "ethnic minority" and "ethnically Danish"? We should also examine how the term "immigrant" is used in comparison to the term "expat." While a white person who has immigrated to Denmark from, for instance, the US or Germany is typically referred to as an "expat" or an "international," we tend to refer to a person of color who has immigrated from, for instance, Senegal or Pakistan as an "immigrant." Both are immigrants who may have moved to Denmark on their own initiative or due to their job situation. However, they are racialized quite differently; one of them will likely be classified as belonging to a "minority ethnic group," while the other will not be, and our stereotypical assumptions about them will shift accordingly. As mentioned earlier, the terms "Western" and "non-Western" are also racialized, as it is not the geographical location on a map that determines whether the country is considered Western or non-Western but whether the majority group of people (in power) are European (or have immigrated from Europe)—that is, white.

On the basis of these considerations, I prefer to use the terms "racialized minority" and "racialized majority" in the context of discrimination based on race and ethnicity; however, when I draw on statistical studies, I will use the words used by these studies and the national registers they draw on—for example, "Western" and "non-Western" or "black," "brown," "person of color," and "white."

Racial discrimination is clearly a highly complex issue, but it is paramount that we do not ignore (or deny) its existence, as research undeniably shows the pervasiveness of discrimination based on skin color and the racialization of identity in Nordic workplaces. In Denmark, 20% of wage earners with an ethnic minority background report having experienced racial discrimination in the workplace,[11] and 25% of Danish citizens with so-called non-Western backgrounds have, within the last two years, been refused admittance to places where other people have been allowed to enter, such as buses, cabs, or nightclubs.[12] In both American and European CV studies, similar to those mentioned above, it has been demonstrated that having a so-called non-Western sounding name means that you have to send up to 50% more applications before being invited to an interview. It is simply not possible to assess a person's skills without being influenced by their presumed racialized identity. Since the CVs in these studies do not even include a picture, only two different names, the studies solely measure the racialization associated with different names—for example, Mohamad versus Mads in a Danish study, Ali versus Erik in a Swedish study, and Jamal versus Greg in an American study. Further documentation of this racialization comes from a recent Danish study[13] that asked 1264 primary school teachers if they had room for one more pupil in their respective classes. A short description of the pupil was attached. The descriptions were completely identical; however, half of the teachers were told that the pupil was named Mathias, while the other half received a description in which the pupil was named Yousef. Who do you think the primary school teachers had room for in their classes? Unfortunately, but not surprisingly, many more were willing to accommodate Mathias compared to Yousef.

Lately, vocational education has been on the Danish public agenda, particularly the opportunities for apprentices to find apprenticeships. In 2023, the Danish Institute for Human Rights conducted a study among vocational colleges' student counselors, in which the counselors were asked how often organizations would have specific demands for the ethnicity of students when looking for apprentices. Of the respondents, 36% said that they would "often" or "sometimes" encounter organizations with specific demands or expectations regarding the ethnicity of apprentices, while only 20% said that they had never experienced such demands. What may be most surprising, however, is that 51% of the student counselors who had been asked to accommodate the (illegal) demands regarding the ethnicity of students had, in fact, tried to do so.

Discrimination based on sexual orientation and gender identity

Sexual orientation and gender identity are relevant identity dimensions to consider in relation to gender and race/ethnicity, as these two dimensions, compared to the others, are more subtle and often invisible. However, before we delve into the research on this type of discrimination, it is once again important to consider the terminology.

Sexual orientation indicates who one is romantically, emotionally, and/or sexually attracted to, whereas gender identity indicates the gender one identifies with. To simplify this somewhat, in the acronym LGBTQ+, L, G, and B stand for lesbian, gay, and bisexual, respectively, and represent sexual orientations. In contrast, T and Q indicate gender identities[14]; T stands for transgender, and Q stands for queer. The latter covers a broad spectrum of fluid gender identities, including the non-binary label. Queer identities all challenge the binary (male/female) perception of gender, and it is now widely acknowledged that sexual orientation and gender identity are not inherently connected. Furthermore, the + in LGBTQ+ indicates that many more sexual orientations and gender identities exist, many of which have their own acronyms—for instance, A for asexual, P for pansexual, I for intersex, and 2 for two-spirit. The two-spirit identity is particularly common in the North American context, where it is associated with indigenous or first nation people and, hence, intersects with race and ethnicity. As in the case of the broader identity dimensions, no matter how long a list we make of different sexual orientations and gender identities, there will always be more that could and should be included.

A common cause of everyday discrimination against LGBTQ+ people is that many people do not know the difference between gender identity and sexual orientation. However, these two dimensions do not depend on each other, and they can intersect in many different ways. For instance, a lesbian woman can identify as cisgender (meaning that she identifies with the gender she was assigned at birth), both before and after coming out as a lesbian. On the contrary, a transgender woman (a woman who was assigned male at birth but identifies as a woman) could always have been attracted to women, which means that she would previously have been perceived as heterosexual (because her surroundings perceived her as male) but is now perceived as a lesbian. This also means that having sex reassignment surgery in itself does not influence a person's sexual orientation and that stereotypical assumptions can in themselves be hurtful (e.g., "butch lesbian," "feminine trans woman," etc.).

With the basic terminology in place, we can now explore how LGBTQ+ people experience discrimination in the workplace. It is important to acknowledge that this type of everyday discrimination can be very difficult to talk about because it is about sexuality—or coded as being about sexuality. Therefore, many people think of it as a private or intimate topic that does not belong in the workplace. For example, I cannot count the number of times I have been told that who people are romantically involved with is completely irrelevant in a work context. The people who say this may be right; maybe it should be irrelevant. The problem is that heterosexual involvement is always present, even when we do not notice it.

To give an example, consider two male colleagues who, on a Monday morning, are talking about their respective weekends. Imagine that they share stories about either having been at their holiday homes with their wives or having visited an amusement park with their wives and children. When exchanging this type of everyday information, we also share our sexual orientation (as well as marital, parenthood, and socioeconomic status, among other details), even though most people do not notice it. However, if the two men in the example did not know each other that well and one of them was married to a man, the conversation might be perceived as containing information about sexuality and could turn awkward if one of them were to say, "my husband and I." This person might even refrain from mentioning a partner due to the uncertainty about what reaction it might provoke. Many LGBTQ+ people routinely experience what would otherwise have been everyday conversation taking a different turn when they are met with comments such as "oh, I did not see that coming"; "that is OK!"; or "my brother is gay too!" What started out as a casual conversation about weekend plans is now a confessional conversation about sexual orientation (or gender identity). The reactions are not necessarily hostile (however, these also occur, as shown below), but in most cases, they still need to be handled or contained emotionally. Often, it is the person who has "revealed" something about themselves who is expected to handle their conversational partner's response in a way that restores the pleasant atmosphere. However, we may ask who is actually responsible for "sexualizing" the conversation. To assess whether a reaction is appropriate, one could imagine the same things being said to the two heterosexual men mentioned above. If a man is talking about his wife, can you imagine someone responding with "oh, I did not realize that you were straight"; "that is OK!"; or "my brother is also straight"? Not really, right?

To avoid "making trouble," many LGBTQ+ people choose to keep their sexual orientation or gender identity to themselves. In fact, a Boston

Consulting Group study shows that 40% of LGBTQ+ people are not open about their sexual orientation or gender identity at work. This may not seem like a problem because, supposedly, these people just talk about something else. However, consider how much heterosexual people engage in small talk that involves their partners, connecting with each other and creating familiarity. Now try to imagine how much energy it takes to keep your private life hidden by avoiding talking about it and consider how people who do not discuss their private lives are perceived by their colleagues—at best introverted and at worst insincere?

Furthermore, it can be difficult for many LGBTQ+ people to determine if and when they should mention their partner and thus "come out." If done too soon, it is often criticized as unnecessary information, with comments such as "gay people always have to flaunt their sexual orientation." However, if people do not mention the gender identity of their partner, they are most often assumed to be heterosexual (as in Martin's story in the preface), and if someone corrects this normative assumption later, it is often considered this person's responsibility to handle the other person's response, relieving them of their confusion, awkwardness, or whatever feelings emerge. Furthermore, people who do not have a partner are often assumed to be heterosexual until proven otherwise.

Discrimination based on sexual orientation or gender identity tends to be more frequent and more difficult to identify and handle because these dimensions are often invisible or ambiguous. Many heterosexual people do not even realize the true extent of the LGBTQ+ population. The Danish Institute for Human Rights estimates that one out of ten people in Denmark identifies as LGBTQ+, and this number is only increasing with younger generations' rejection of binary gender norms.[15] However, if only 40% are out at work, and perhaps only to a small group of close colleagues who know about their private lives, then most workplaces have LGBTQ+ people who do not feel safe about sharing parts of themselves that other people consider so normal to share that they do not even notice sharing them. This also means that most workplaces have heterosexual people who think they have no LGBTQ+ colleagues.

Most people view Denmark as a safe place to identify as LGBTQ+. Many even think that LGBTQ+ initiatives in Denmark are no longer necessary because it is legal and commonly accepted to be an LGBTQ+ person. However, this illustrates the circularity of discrimination, as described above. Given that circumstances are better in Denmark compared to countries in which homosexuality is still illegal and may even be punishable by death, one may think that Denmark has achieved complete equity and that LGBTQ+ people have no more battles to fight. Unfortunately, research shows that

37% of the Danish population reports having experienced LGBTQ+ people being talked about derogatorily in their workplaces. In addition, according to a survey conducted by ALS Research,[16] 12% of the surveyed LGB individuals had experienced negative comments or behavior related to their sexual orientation within the last year. Furthermore, 23% of the surveyed transgender people had experienced negative comments or behavior related to their gender identity within the last year. Despite the aforementioned negative consequences of not being open about one's sexual orientation or gender identity at work, 7% of the LGB individuals and 25% of the transgender individuals surveyed stated that they had regretted instances of "coming out" within the last two years. Finally, 10% of the LGB individuals and 34% of the transgender individuals stated that they had changed jobs because they could not be themselves at work.

Intersectional discrimination

As previously mentioned, many more identity dimensions exist, and these can all become subject to discrimination. It is particularly important to mention that, in addition to the three that I have described above, age, disability, and religion are also covered by the antidiscrimination legislation in Denmark. Another important point to remember is that none of these identities exist in a vacuum. They affect each other in ways that research seeks to explain through the lens of intersectionality.

Put simply, intersectionality means that different identity dimensions overlap or cut across each other and, therefore, affect how each is perceived and experienced, alone and in combination (or, perhaps more precisely, that we never experience one dimension alone but are always affected by the combination). Thus, the type and amount of discrimination experienced change according to perceived intersectionalities. The concept of intersectionality was popularized in 1989 by legal scholar Kimberly Crenshaw, who used it to describe the double discrimination that black women experience. They experience discrimination based on both gender and race, and as these forms of discrimination intersect in complex ways that are "more" than the simple addition of the two, it is difficult to fight the combined discrimination using the same (legal) means. Sexism and racism influence each other, but they have different meanings; therefore, they can also influence each other differently in different contexts. Crenshaw, for example, argued that black women experience racism differently than black men and also experience sexism differently than white women. This is why the "-isms" cannot just be multiplied; rather, the discrimination that an individual experiences must be considered at the intersection between these "-isms."

Since Crenshaw's popular article, intersectionality as a concept has been utilized in professional and social contexts to examine how various other identities intersect and thus affect each other. For instance, we know that many people experience age discrimination and that it can be difficult for people over fifty-five to change jobs. However, if we consider age and gender intersectionally, research shows that both younger and older women experience more age discrimination in the job market than men in the same age brackets. Younger women are not taken seriously in the same way younger men are, and older men are not considered "as old" as older women. In addition, research shows that the sexism women experience changes in character as they age. While younger women are subject to more sexualized comments, the sexism older women experience is aimed more at their intellect and personality. This illustrates that sexism and ageism also cannot "just" be multiplied; rather, such forms of discrimination must be analyzed within their specific intersections.

In Denmark (as in many other contexts), both in society and the workplace, there exists extensive Islamophobia—that is, discrimination against Muslims. Islamophobia is present in everyday life in the form of comments, jokes, and ridicule (as in Mehmet's case in the preface) but also in more hostile forms of discrimination, such as being spat on or yelled at in the street. In this way, Islamophobia amplifies discrimination based on race, and if we combine gender with race and religious beliefs, yet another dimension emerges. Here, we can see how prominent religious symbols, such as hijabs (head scarves) or turbans, increase the amount of discrimination that people experience. The aforementioned

CV method has been used to capture this as well; studies of CVs with pictures show that women with hijabs have to send 60% more applications before they are called for an interview compared to people who look "Danish" (i.e., white and Christian). In an experimental study that measured the difference in hostile comments directed at people standing on the "wrong" side of an escalator, it was found that there was significantly more hostility when the subject was wearing a hijab compared to when she was not. In a similar study, when women with hijabs asked to borrow a phone for an emergency call, they would face refusals more often compared to women who did not wear hijabs.

Finally, research has found intersectional effects on wage gaps. When we discuss wage gaps, most people would (rightly) think about a gender wage gap that disadvantages women. In fact, according to Statistics Denmark, the wage gap between men and women in the Danish labor market was 13.5% in 2022. However, if we consider migrant status along with gender, we can see an intersectional effect: Men who have immigrated to Denmark from a so-called non-Western country but have completed their higher education in Denmark make 8.4% less than their Danish male colleagues, whereas women who have immigrated to Denmark from a so-called non-Western country but have completed their higher education in Denmark "only" make 3.1% less than their Danish female colleagues. In essence, the advantage of being a man is lessened by having a non-Western immigrant status.

Common characteristics of everyday discrimination

As previously mentioned, everyday discrimination often goes unnoticed, but what does this mean? How can we identify that which is submerged in our everyday interactions? To answer these questions, I identify five characteristics that are found in all dimensions and differentiate everyday discrimination from other types of discrimination.

First, everyday discrimination is often vague, subtle, and/or concealed in everyday conversations, jokes and humor, casual comments, jargon, and "tone" that have been normalized in the workplace culture. While these types of comments can be relatively unproblematic, they are often more discriminatory and less "fun" when they are directed at or about an underrepresented or marginalized group. It is also important to remember that we all have different boundaries; hence, what is funny to one person may be discriminatory to another, even if they share the same nominal identity position. Mehmet's story from the beginning of this book is a clear example of how everyday discrimination can be vague. His more experienced colleague is used to a harsher tone at the construction site, where crude jokes create a sense of solidarity between the team members. The problem is that, in this particular workplace, the sense of solidarity is primarily created among white men. The colleague is used to laughing at jokes about skin color, religion, or women with other people who look like himself, which is why he may not take the joke as seriously as Mehmet does. It is not directed at him and not about something that makes him "different" from the others. He does not think that it is so "serious." However, a joke always hits harder when it is about a group that one is part of, particularly if a historical hierarchy exists, such as the one between racialized groups. This is also why harsh comments among in-group members (in this case, the white male colleagues) rarely hurt as much as when these comments are directed at a colleague who is not part of this in-group. Thus, it is also important to recognize the role power plays in the relationship; the racist ideology that has produced a power disparity between white people and non-white people in most societies is also at play in the example involving Mehmet. Their racialized inequalities are aggravated by their hierarchical positions within the organization.

Jokes and humor always seem less offensive (and funnier) from the dominant position. The person in power may not even realize that a comment is problematic, whereas the one on the receiving end of the comment (and who it may even be about) can feel very vulnerable and unsafe. Due to this uneven balance of power, everyday discrimination is also described as microaggressions, a term that emphasizes how what seems minor to some can be regarded as aggressive and unpleasant by others.

The second characteristic of everyday discrimination is that it is often difficult to ascribe it to one specific situation. Because of its subtleness, a comment or an action of everyday discrimination is typically not all that problematic on its own. If a person has only heard the comment once in their life, they may not even notice it. Rather, the discriminating effect comes from repetition, which is what makes such discrimination structural. Turning to Mehmet's experience with his colleague once again, we can assume he might not have thought much of it (or might just have found the comment odd) if he had never been racialized through derogatory comments or heard jokes about his religion before. Unfortunately, it is very likely that Mehmet has heard such jokes before, as multiple studies show that racialized minorities in general hear such comments often. If it had been the first time Mehmet had heard such a joke, he probably would not have felt so unsafe, as it would not have played into the likely experience that he is rarely safe from discrimination in the company of mostly white colleagues. In sum, it is not the singular isolated situation that is problematic. It may even, with a certain amount of goodwill, pass as a joke. However, hearing stereotypes repeated again and again by different people and in different ways turns jokes into structural discrimination.

My co-authors of the book *Sexism in Danish Higher Education and Research*[17] and I have called this phenomenon the drip-drip effect. It is not a single isolated drop but the accumulated effect of the total number of drops that makes the cup run over. In the same way, a joke about blondes that demeans women's intellect might not be considered problematic if it was only ever said once. One might not even remember it. However, if this type of joke is repeated again and again in a workplace, it establishes a norm implying that women in general and blonde women in particular do not have the skills necessary to be taken seriously or pursue a career in that workplace. What makes everyday discrimination so difficult to handle is not only that it can be unclear and vague but also the fact that it is so pervasive. Consequently, it is difficult to confront. If one decides to make a complaint about a specific situation, say a joke, because they find it inappropriate, the complaint may very easily be trivialized or brushed aside. Hence, the person making the complaint may risk being considered "sensitive" or unable to "take a joke." However, if a person decides to stay silent about a specific issue, they can later be accused of having waited "too long" and of not having taken the appropriate action and stood up for themselves in time. This makes it difficult to know when "enough is enough," and people who experience everyday discrimination always run the risk of speaking up either too soon or too late. It is very difficult to find the right time between the drops.

The third characteristic of everyday discrimination is that it often draws on deeply rooted societal norms about gender, race, religion, sexual orientation, age, and other identity markers that are internalized as attitudes and opinions in each and every one of us. As a result, it is difficult to distinguish discriminatory actions from warranted assumptions. For instance, regarding gender norms, society has "taught" its members for centuries that men are efficient, proactive, and dedicated providers, while women are gentle, attentive, and selfless caregivers. This perception is still deeply rooted in most of us today, stored in our subconscious, despite recent decades' persistent focus on gender equality. We can, for example, see this in our inclination to find managerial skills in men and administrative skills in women or our tendency to expect women to have children (and be their primary caregivers) and men to not be involved in childcare to an extent that affects their performance at work. The example of Peter in the preface draws on a norm that implies that men are sexually active, while women are sexually passive. This is why his uneasiness with the female student's behavior is not taken seriously. On the contrary, he is ridiculed, despite the fact that his experience, legally speaking, amounts to sexual harassment (as the legal definition includes receiving unwanted pornographic material). Try imagining the exact same situation with the genders reversed. Alternatively, imagine that a male teacher sends pornographic material to a female student.

Why are we more likely to find these two situations transgressive, while Peter's experience was belittled and his reaction ridiculed? The answer lies in how we have normalized and internalized gendered stereotypes that dictate who is strong and who is weak. Of course, women have been rightly accused of and prosecuted for unseemly and transgressive behavior toward men, but these cases are much rarer and much less likely to be taken seriously.

This leads directly to the fourth common characteristic: Everyday discrimination often takes the form of "benevolent discrimination," which is discrimination disguised as praise, compliments, or care. One may even call this well-intentioned discrimination. Because discrimination draws on norms that we are affected by, maybe even without noticing, it is sometimes presented through positive statements. This may sound strange at first, but let us take a look at seemingly harmless scenarios such as praising someone for "speaking Danish so well" or being impressed by a colleague's professional skills "in spite" of them having been trained in India. Such "compliments" draw on a racialized norm that suggests people with a minority-ethnic background are not actually Danish or that they do not have the same skills as Danes. Another type of compliment that can be problematic, particularly if repeated, concerns appearance. Most people do not mind being complimented on their dress or being told that "their shirt is really cool." However, compliments like these can be said in completely different tones of voice, just like glances and body language affect how a compliment is received. The meaning of the same sentence can vary completely depending on the context and articulation. What may be considered a compliment in one instance can be perceived as having sexualized undertones in another, which fosters uncertainty about its intent. This is because sexism is rarely about sex (alone) but (also) about power. If a sentence is said with a sexualized undertone, it becomes a demonstration of power because it reduces the recipient to a body—a sexualized body. These gendered and sexualized comments can be even more hurtful if they are accompanied by a lack of professional acknowledgment. For instance, if a female employee is constantly told that she is good-looking but her male colleague is praised for his performance at work, the norm that says that women are beautiful and that men are competent will be internalized and normalized. As an experiment, think about how often women in your workplace are complimented on their looks and how often men get the same type of compliment. If there is a difference between how men and women are complimented, try to even it out, for instance, by beginning to compliment men more on their looks (if that is the imbalance you identified). If this feels "unnatural" or strange, it is probably because this type of compliment is not appropriate in a professional context in the first place and should not be directed at anyone, regardless of their gender.

Julie's example above is a case of well-intentioned discrimination that emerges from misunderstood care. Julie's organization is experiencing, as many others, female talents leaving the organization in their thirties, when they start having children or have had children for a couple of years. Julie's boss assumes that this may also happen with her, and he tries to avoid that by telling her that he is very keen on keeping her "even when she has children." In this well-intentioned manner, the boss is discriminatory, as he does not even know if Julie wants children. Rather, he assumes this based on the norm, which not only stipulates that women have children but also expects that they prioritize children above their careers. Thus, the boss places Julie at risk of being pushed onto a so-called mommy track—a B-team that gets well-intentioned care but none of the interesting projects or important promotable tasks as well as no credit or consideration for upcoming promotions. Over the years, I have conducted quite a few exit interviews with women in performance-based industries such as consulting. A recurring reason among women for leaving the industry is that they want to be in an organization where they are not seen as "the female employee" who needs special conditions but as an employee like anyone else. It is important to note that Julie's boss also discriminates against Julie's male colleagues, as he is not offering them the same opportunities to prioritize their families. The non-discriminatory solution would have been to communicate the possibility of flexibility to all employees, regardless of their gender or their current or future plans regarding children. This would not only be the most inclusive solution for each individual employee, but the organization would most likely also improve its retention of talented young employees, no matter their gender.

The fifth and final characteristic of everyday discrimination is that it happens both at work and in people's private lives—and that the two cannot be separated. An employee does not come to work with a clean slate when it comes to discrimination. In a workshop I conducted recently, one of the participants, a Danish woman of color, said that it had been less than a week since someone had yelled at her in the street. Several studies show that women, LGBTQ+ people, and racialized minorities regularly experience discrimination in public and from random strangers. People of color are talked down to, yelled at, ignored, or even spat at in the street. Women are sexualized, catcalled, and belittled. LGBTQ+ individuals are subject to violence, threats, and sexualized behavior. Although this happens in people's private lives, they cannot simply leave these experiences behind when they go to work. On the contrary, the feelings they generate are brought into the workplace. The discrimination that people experience in their private lives will inevitably affect how they interpret comments and jokes at work and influence the number of comments they will tolerate from colleagues. If we think of this in terms of the drip-drip effect, it makes sense that the number of recent experiences (and thus a person's general stress level) determines how much an individual can handle—at work as well—before a joke is no longer funny or a comment is perceived as belittling.

Consequences of everyday discrimination

Everyday discrimination is difficult to detect; it often happens latently in subtle everyday situations and is expressed through a normalized everyday tone or register. Nevertheless, it has consequences—rather significant ones, in fact—for the people who experience it. For instance, Danish research shows that LGBTQ+ individuals, racialized minorities, and people with disabilities are more likely to struggle with mental health issues compared to the rest of the population. International studies also establish correlations between experiencing everyday discrimination and alcoholism, emotional instability, increased stress levels, weight gain, sleep deprivation, smoking, depression symptoms, and post-traumatic stress disorder.

The psychological effects of everyday discrimination have been documented by, among others, Iram Khawaja from Aarhus University, who collates them under the umbrella term "minority stress." It is important to emphasize that minority stress, although experienced psychologically, is formed socially. This means that the stress experienced does not come from individual experiences of pressure, as we typically see with other forms of stress, but from the socially constructed norms and behaviors that the individual is influenced by and reacts to. To understand how minority stress works, it is important to bear in mind the fifth characteristic of everyday discrimination, which highlights the interrelationships between people's private and professional lives. Minority stress can arise from experiences at work, but it is often formed from—or reinforced by—experiences in the private and the public sphere. Thus, the drip-drip effect can also help us understand minority stress at work. It is not an isolated episode that provokes a stress reaction, but it can be the last drop that makes the cup run over—and the person break down.

Minority stress, when experienced as constant anxiety, insecurity, or frustration, keeps individuals from living the lives they wish to live. These experiences often cause minority individuals to regulate their behavior in response to actual or anticipated discrimination. In public, one may avoid public transportation and certain neighborhoods or adjust one's appearance or behavior to avoid standing out. At work, people may take a different route to the restroom to avoid certain people, forgo eating lunch or going for coffee—or only do so at certain hours—and evade private conversations; furthermore, they may change their behavior or the way they dress to attract less attention.

Before moving on, it is worth returning to the fact that discrimination affects not only individuals personally but also their job satisfaction and performance. In addition, discrimination and a non-inclusive tone impact not only the individuals concerned but also the entire organizational culture, the level of psychological safety, and, thus, the general well-being and performance in a workplace. A significant amount of the research that I have referred to here presents results at the individual level, as this is how most studies are designed. However, the negative consequences of everyday discrimination extend well beyond the individual (and collections of individuals), as they leave deep structural and institutional scars across our workplaces and societies.

To comprehend the connection between individually experienced discrimination and structural discrimination, it is necessary to take a look at the accumulated effect of individual experiences. Once again, the drip-drip effect is an effective metaphorical lens. A single person being exposed to everyday discrimination (and keep in mind that this is not the extreme, headline-making type of discrimination) is unlikely to leave a trace on the organizational/societal culture. However, because discrimination is created by, emerges from, and is legitimized by sexism, racism, heterosexism, and other ideological "-isms," it is rarely just a single occurrence. As illustrated by both the #MeToo and #BlackLivesMatter movements, this type of discrimination occurs everywhere. When it becomes evident that every single occurrence of a certain type of discrimination can be found in various industries and in all parts of a country (as well as in the rest of the world), it is time to acknowledge that we are dealing with a structurally rooted problem. For the last couple of years, I have been talking to leaders and employees from many different organizations who had difficulties accepting that discrimination was real prior to #MeToo and #BlackLivesMatter. However, after seeing discrimination substantiated by the abundance of testimonies, they have realized that discrimination is everywhere. They now accept that comments about a female candidate's "way of being" or a female employee's "lacking will" are not neutral but are, in fact, expressions of structural sexism. Similarly, most people now realize that the candidate with a Middle Eastern background who does not ask for a particularly high salary is probably not any less serious about their job than anyone else. More likely, they are used to being rejected and are trying to signal that they really want the job. In addition, many people can now better see that the candidate wearing a hijab was rejected not due to inadequate qualifications but because the manager was scared of "taking a risk." When we gather all these examples, an appalling pattern emerges. This is why we must recognize everyday discrimination at the individual and the structural level to fight it effectively.

Status:
Policies and
minority focus

Status: Policies and minority focus

As discrimination is destructive, both to the individual's mental health and the organization's performance, most workplaces wish to fight it. However, there are not many who know how to do so, and unfortunately, most of the initiatives that are currently implemented have limited effect, particularly when it comes to everyday discrimination. In the following sections, I present the most common ways in which organizations try to fight everyday discrimination; subsequently, I explain why they have little effect. The efforts that currently dominate can be divided into four categories: zero tolerance, voluntariness, minority initiatives, and bias training. These are all detailed below.

Zero tolerance

In an attempt to prevent discrimination and create an inclusive organizational culture, most organizations have implemented policies, protocols, and standards for how their employees are expected to behave and treat each other. However, these rarely have an effect when it comes to everyday discrimination, as it is incredibly difficult to agree on rules about what is considered acceptable behavior among colleagues. Of course, an organization should have policies, protocols, and standards that affirm that it does not accept discrimination, and these should specify the processes available if an employee is feeling discriminated against or is experiencing harassment. Unfortunately, because everyday discrimination can be so difficult to detect and because boundaries vary from person to person and from situation to situation, it is very difficult to determine when to apply said policies, protocols, and standards. It goes without saying that management should always articulate zero tolerance for anything illegal and criminal. However, if we refer to the stories at the beginning of this book, it is difficult to see how rules and zero tolerance could have prevented them from happening.

The fact that zero tolerance often fails to apply to everyday discrimination is not the only shortcoming of this strategy. Another is that it tends to shut down dialogues—and dialogues are necessary to increase our understanding of what constitutes and who is impacted by discriminatory actions. For instance, in the stories in the preface, none of the protagonists have a clear idea about boundaries (neither their own nor those of others'), what is and is not considered humor, how certain words would be perceived by others, or how to stand up for themselves (or even whether to stand up for themselves). By declaring zero tolerance toward everyday discrimination in an organization, you risk shutting down conversations about all these aspects that we find difficult. It is extremely important to have honest and constructive (and difficult) conversations about gray zones, individual boundaries, and what is and is not considered funny, as well as about how we are all affected differently by all of these factors. We all have different boundaries, but we have to be able to talk about them and acknowledge what feels right and wrong to each other; only then will it be possible to speak up whenever we feel that a personal boundary is being crossed.

As Katy Greenland and colleagues found in 2018, policies and protocols are, unfortunately, a lot more effective at showing what is *not* discriminatory behavior than they are at directing attention to what is. The burden of proof usually lies with the wronged; thus, if it cannot be proven that an incident broke the rules, it is typically concluded that the incident was not a case of discrimination. This is why policies and protocols often end up silencing the problem or sweeping it under the rug; people eventually give up on the formal reporting systems with which they have bad experiences. Policies and protocols may help identify the extreme cases of a few "bad apples," but they are not great at solving the problem at its root—the structural level, where we need to discuss which norms are problematic as well as when and how to change them. In other words, policies and protocols are effective in instances of explicit and overt discrimination, whereas they may actually obstruct the identification and handling of everyday discrimination.

Voluntariness

The notion of voluntariness covers two dynamics. First, more often than not, diversity initiatives in the workplace are initiated by passionate volunteers and volunteering work groups rather than strategically driven by top management. Second, training in how to fight everyday discrimination is usually voluntary and not part of the organization's mandatory employee development.

Let us first take a look at the way in which most organizations' DEI and antidiscrimination initiatives are run by passionate volunteers. These volunteers are typically organized as employee resource groups (ERCs) that are mandated to provide management with information about minorities' experiences, diversity committees that serve as advisory organs, or informal employee networks that serve as support systems or safe spaces for minoritized employees. Employees often join these different voluntary bodies because they are familiar with discrimination, either because they are part of a minority themselves or because they have family members or close friends who are. This means that there is considerable emotional investment in the work done by these groups. Obviously, it is not the commitment in itself that is problematic but the fact that, without strategic (top management) support or resources, volunteers will often feel as if they are banging their heads against a brick wall. If they do so one too many times, they may stop trying entirely.

The British-Australian author and researcher Sara Ahmed vividly describes voluntary diversity work in the book *On Being Included*. In it, she discusses how working for the DEI and antidiscrimination agenda can lead to immense affective strain in the form of fatigue, anger, and frustration because the participants do not feel included in the organization but are positioned against it as a result of their voluntariness. Voluntary groups can be amazing, and they can bring a lot of good energy to very important work, but it is crucial that they are supported and acknowledged by the organization's top management—not only verbally but also through participation, resources, and initiatives that obligate the entire organization to uphold its diversity commitments. Far too often, I have seen passionate employees doing an amazing job, outside office hours and financed by themselves. Ultimately, this is what leads to burnout.

The next problematic aspect is that it is often voluntary to participate in antidiscrimination courses or courses, events, and seminars on more general themes of diversity and inclusion, and it does not help that these often come in the form of webinars or short presentations. Consequently, many people, including those who need the training the most, are able to ignore the agenda. If an organization truly wants to fight everyday discrimination, it is necessary to engage in a thorough and comprehensive discussion about the type of workplace it would like to foster as well as how its employees should treat each other.

In the next chapter, I lay out the design of such a process. For now, the point is that it should not be voluntary to participate. If it is not part of the organization's mandatory training, the only people who will show up are the ones who already recognize the problem. If we do not succeed in getting the rest—the ones who have not yet realized the problem or even the ones who are causing or perpetuating the problem—on board, we cannot create organizational and structural change.

Minority initiatives

When organizations begin to address discrimination and attempt to create more focus on DEI, they often begin with minority initiatives, such as talent programs for women with managerial potential, trainee programs aimed at enrolling more racialized minorities, or LGBT networks that, for instance, organize Pride participation. Although initiatives like these can add a certain value to an organization, if they are not accompanied by other initiatives that are directed at the organization's norms and culture, they risk drawing even more attention to specific people's differences and marginalizing certain employees further. Ultimately, they risk amplifying prevailing stereotypes about women, racialized minorities, and LGBTQ+ individuals not being the "ideal employees."

Furthermore, minority initiatives tend to individualize the problem by focusing on minorities' abilities to speak up. Unfortunately, when it comes to everyday discrimination, this can be incredibly difficult: How does one fight something that is vague and casual, embedded in the culture and normalized to the point of being commonly accepted? We have to be very careful not to individualize the problem. Instead of placing the burden on minority individuals, we must acknowledge the structural and institutional character of everyday discrimination and learn to handle its consequences collectively.

Bias training

Many organizations have realized that unconscious bias produces everyday discrimination in the workplace. This is also why several organizations have started offering different forms of bias training, mostly as (voluntary) online courses, webinars, or short workshops. These are all steps in the right direction—a direction toward an active fight against everyday discrimination in the workplace. However, research shows that this type of training does not have an impact on its own. The problem is that becoming aware of our bias and the everyday discrimination happening around us does not automatically lead to change. If this awareness is not accompanied by the development and implementation of strategies for avoiding discrimination and blocking bias, people are often at a loss as to how to handle their new knowledge. Consequently, they are left feeling bad about their privileges rather than encouraged to use them to fight structural discrimination. They may seek to compensate by trying to be inclusive but can end up practicing well-intentioned discrimination instead because they do not have the right tools. In brief, it can be said that bias training does not work if it is not supported by the development of tools and methods that are both geared toward action and tailored to the individual organizational context.

Change: You, me, and all of us

Change: You, me, and all of us

Knowledge, attitude, and behavior

Bias training on its own does not work. Either the effect disappears shortly after the training, or it might even create backlash as majorities seek to deal with feelings of guilt while possessing no means of acting on them. So how do we fight everyday discrimination effectively and with a permanent effect? In our book *Leading Through* Bias, my colleague Poornima Luthra and I adopt the knowledge-attitude-behavior (KAB) framework. We begin by establishing that the prerequisite for fighting everyday discrimination is a solid knowledge base (the K). Personal experience and feelings are not enough. To become better at identifying everyday discrimination, it is important to acquire knowledge about the different types of everyday discrimination that we experience at work.

However, it is not enough to use our rationally gained knowledge either. After attending a presentation on everyday discrimination, or when reading this book, most people will probably agree that discrimination has no place at work—or anywhere else in society, for that matter—and many people will also be able to describe its characteristics. However, the process often stops there, as people tend to forget about the issue as soon as the wheels of everyday life (and work) are set back in motion. This is why the first step of increasing people's rational knowledge base is not enough; we also have to experience discrimination at an emotional level. When feelings are evoked (e.g., shame, anger, grief, joy, sadness, etc.), the will to fight everyday discrimination is more likely to remain, despite the pressures and distractions of work. Far too often, the DEI agenda is pushed aside to make room for something that seems more important and urgent. This is because there has not been a change in attitude (the A), as the feeling of necessity has not emerged.

However, this is still not enough. If we stop here, what happens is that people easily get overwhelmed by the amount of injustice they are experiencing. They simply cannot cope with having to do anything about it, as it seems too much. Furthermore, when the problem is also identified as a structural and institutionalized issue that calls for a change in culture, then, surely, it is out of our hands; how does anyone instigate cultural change? To address this question, we need the final step—behavior (the B). This is essential if we are to attain any permanent effect. Studies show that change only happens when people are offered concrete actions that they can make use of. Importantly, however, such actions cannot be regarded as "one-size-fits-all" solutions but need to be adjusted to and tested within the specific context. In the following sections, I present a range of methods that can be utilized to go from knowledge to attitude and from attitude to behavior. These will hopefully be sources of inspiration for you and your organization, but remember that they need to be tailored to your specific situation and context.[18]

From the individual to the collective and the collegial

When fighting everyday discrimination, we must recognize it as a structural and institutionalized problem that demands collective action. This involves several aspects.

First, we must stop trying to "fix the minority." It is not the minority that has to accommodate other people's discomfort, learn how to take a joke, or leave if they do not like it here. It is the majority that must, intentionally and actively, take steps to create more inclusive workplaces. If we individualize the problem, we merely increase the potential for minority stress, allowing structural discrimination to become even more manifest *and* ingrained.

The #MeToo and #BlackLivesMatter movements have created awareness of the fact that discrimination is not about single occurrences but permeates our institutions and workplaces. While this has encouraged people to speak up, it has also illustrated that everyday discrimination is a collective problem. Furthermore, it has brought attention to how change can happen only through collective action.

The acknowledgment of systemic discrimination has also made it possible to direct critical attention to the fact that discrimination often occurs in large groups (e.g., workplaces and other organizations) in which a silent majority witnesses discrimination passively, without contributing to it directly but also without countering it in any way. We saw this clearly in many #MeToo stories, in which people said they had witnessed episodes that made them uncomfortable but still did not feel they could interfere or did not know how to do so. We may all be inspired by the victims' courage to speak up, but it is the silent majority that holds the key to permanent change. If we all were to stand up for others and for the values that we believe in, we would, little by little, unravel the closely woven structural net of everyday discrimination. In contrast, when no one (leaders or colleagues) speaks up, unsafe and unhealthy working environments emerge and endure.

In other words, for collective action to work, everyone must become an active ally. Being an ally means that a privileged group's members support and verbalize minorities' issues and help them gain access to influential networks and other organizational resources. We can all be allies in some way or another. Even if you are part of a minority group, you are still likely to have privileges in other areas—privileges that can be utilized to fight and speak up for others. To shift the focus from the minority to the majority, all of us must take a good look at ourselves, identify the areas in which we are particularly privileged, and explore how we can use that privilege to help others.

It is—and *should* be—difficult

It is not easy to start a collective movement against discrimination. Then again, it is not supposed to be. If we really want to be able to talk about everyday discrimination, be it sexism, racism, heterosexism, or any of the other several sources of everyday discrimination that create an unsafe working environment and minority stress in the workplace, we must have the courage and strength to begin vulnerable conversations filled with insecurities, guilt, and discomfort. Furthermore, it is crucial that we sit with these insecurities without rushing back to more comfortable and easy topics. Luckily, we have different means of making these conversations a little easier. Below, I walk you through one of them: the vignette technique.[19]

Vignettes are stories that are based on multiple people's true personal accounts, woven together to ensure that they can never be traced back to just one individual. An organization can collect anonymous stories about its employees' experiences with everyday discrimination. This can be done using the following prompt: "Tell us about an experience in which you have felt different, excluded, and/or unsafe." The stories should be handed in anonymously. Subsequently, they must be systematically read and thematically coded to identify common features and to develop a series of vignettes that cover these. The resultant vignettes are based on multiple real stories that have been combined and/or otherwise altered. Hence, individual employees are protected, but the stories still serve as realistic examples of everyday discrimination in the organization.

Each vignette should be accompanied by questions that can facilitate a discussion of it. The questions should include emotive/empathic elements as well as action-oriented aspects (to cover the K, A, and B of antidiscrimination work). Such questions can include "why do you think that the narrator is uncomfortable in this situation?" and "have you ever felt uncomfortable in a situation like this one?" When people are probed via these questions, they are encouraged to relate personally to the stories they are presented with. The aim is to ensure that people are not just made aware of the dynamics presented in the vignettes but that they also genuinely feel their importance and the necessity of acting to address them. The vignettes also aim to make it possible for people to be open about their own experiences, if they feel safe enough to do so. Another person's story being the center of attention may make it easier to choose how much one wants to share about one's own experiences.

Empathy-oriented questions are followed by action-oriented ones, such as "what can you, as a colleague, do in this situation?" and "what do you think management should do in order to avoid or handle a similar situation in the future?" The aim of discussing the vignettes is to both address how discrimination can be found within the organization and explore how you can fight it together.

If an organization does not have the resources or the time to produce its own vignettes, resources can be found elsewhere. For instance, you can refer to the book *Sexism in Higher Education and Research*, which is based on more than 900 testimonies collected at Danish universities during the #MeToo wave in the fall of 2020.[20] Alternatively, you can begin with the four vignettes that I have presented at the outset and used throughout this book.

Everyday inclusion

While fundamental and enduring changes do require a certain level of organizational and managerial action, there are also minor initiatives that individual employees can apply to change the culture in their workplace. Acting can, indeed, seem overwhelming if the only way to create structural change is when management initiates sweeping processes. Management initiatives are necessary, but change can happen at the level of everyday interaction and can be motivated by colleagues as well. Below, I present a series of everyday actions that anyone can practice, regardless of their position in the organization. If more people use these, we can collectively inspire broader processes and begin to reduce structural discrimination.

A more inclusive tone begins with you

If you want a more inclusive tone in your workplace, you must start with how you speak. For instance, get used to asking open-ended questions—that is, questions in which you do not unintentionally assume a person's sexual orientation, parental or partnership status, or place of birth but instead make it possible for the other person to freely give this type of information if they wish to. Instead of asking your female colleague if she has any children or what her husband does, try to ask her what she did on the weekend. This way, she gets to choose what information she wants to share. If she tells you that she went to a vacation home with her partner and you would like to know more about the partner, you could, for instance, ask her, "What does your partner do?" instead of asking, "Where does *he* work?" In other words, do not use the partner's pronouns until she has told you what they are (and do not assume she has a partner if her story about her weekend does not include one). Furthermore, instead of asking a colleague who belongs to a racialized minority group where they are from, you could ask if they have always been interested in computers (or whatever it is you work with or talk about at lunch), allowing them to share a story about the teacher at their primary school in their hometown who introduced them to programming (or give you any other information about themselves that they deem relevant). If this information involves facts about having grown up in another country, then you can ask about that or when they moved. If they tell you that they grew up in Copenhagen, Amsterdam, or Frankfurt, do not ask where they are "originally" from, as this would communicate to them that the way they look signals foreignness to you (that is, you racialize them as different in ways you would not have done with a white person), and this will most likely make them feel excluded and cause minority stress.

Call out everyday discrimination, respectfully

Practice not staying silent. Call out everyday discrimination. However, everyday discrimination always happens when we least expect it, which is why it is often when we are on our way home that we think of what we *should* have said. Thus, to make it easier to react on the spot, you can have a few sentences ready. A good strategy is to reply with a question. For instance, you can say some version of "why do you say that?"; "what do you mean by that?"; or "why do you find this funny?" You can even pretend to be a bit slow and say, "Sorry, I don't get why this is funny. Can you please explain it to me?" This takes the burden of explanation away from you (or the receiver of the comment, if it is not addressed to you directly) and places it back on the person who made the remark. If you witness everyday discrimination, you can (and often should) intervene, but make sure to draw attention to yourself without making assumptions about how others feel. For instance, you could say, "I do not like it when you generalize about our international colleagues like that," "I get uncomfortable when you speak about Adam that way," or "I would like to hear what Maria is saying; would you let her continue?"

Build alliances with others

Create support networks with your close colleagues in which you promise to help each other if any of you experience everyday discrimination. Verbalize what you find uncomfortable and what makes you feel unsafe. Agree that all of you will pay attention and react if and when these situations occur. If you speak up for your colleague, your colleague speaks up for you, or, even better, you speak up together, your message will be much more powerful.

Ask yourself and others reverse questions

If you often overhear generalizations or you make them yourself, try asking yourself—and others—a reverse question. Reverse questions are based on a version of "would I/we/you have said the same thing or said it in the same way if it had been aimed at a man and not a woman?" Of course, "man" and "woman" can be replaced with other generalized binaries, such as "white person" and "person of color"; "heterosexual person" and "homosexual person"; or "old" and "young." If the answer is "no," your opinion or remark is probably an example of normalized discrimination based on stereotypes and bias. For example, would you note if a man was not smiling much at a job interview, or would you ask a heterosexual person if they had always been straight? Realizing the inappropriateness of the assumption or question may help you avoid making similar statements in the future (or stop you from making them in the first place).

Make your meetings more inclusive

Meetings are a regular activity in most workplaces, and during these, it is typically the same people who are speaking (first). Research shows that majority members usually speak the most, thus disadvantaging minoritized individuals. However, it is very rare that those who stay silent have nothing to contribute. Therefore, it is a great idea (for both individuals and the decision-making processes in the organization) to work actively toward hosting meetings in which more (or a broader variety of) people get to say something.

If you are a smaller group, you can take turns speaking, and if you also swap seats between meetings, maybe even by placing name tags around the table, you can change the order in which people get to speak. If you are a bigger group, you can write down your points on post-it notes and hang them on the wall so that the meeting facilitator can pick out random post-it notes that you can all discuss. You can also start off by talking in pairs or in smaller groups to get people going. It may still be the people in majority positions and/or the more senior, confident, and extroverted people who present to the rest of the group, but at least they now represent others and not just themselves.

Invite quiet colleagues to participate in the conversation

If you have a colleague who rarely says anything, try asking them why that is. If it is because they do not like talking in front of everyone, you may be able to help. If you agree beforehand what the person should say and you promise to be the first person to comment that "that's a great idea!" and possibly continue the discussion from there, you may be able to remove some of the insecurity about speaking up that the quiet colleague is feeling, as well as removing the attention from them after they have spoken. This could enable their active participation in meetings.

Be an active ally

Many organizations have mentor programs. These can be great, but they can also lead to well-intentioned discrimination if the bulk of the program involves the mentor telling the mentee to do as they have done in order to become as successful as them. Instead, try to become an "active ally." Regardless of your position in the organization, you can make an active effort to identify a person in your organization who is part of a less privileged or underrepresented group compared to you and engage in acts of active allyship to lift this person up. The premise of active allyship is to identify the discrimination that this person may be enduring and to take action to circumvent this, as opposed to changing the person. The difference between being someone's mentor and being an active ally is that a mentor gives advice (with the purpose of changing or developing the mentee), whereas an active ally makes an effort to remove the barriers that this person may be encountering in the organization due to their minority identity. The acts of active allyship do not have to be grand; they can be as simple as asking someone to join you for lunch, bringing them to an important networking event, or even simply talking positively about their competencies or accomplishments to managers.[21] It could also involve standing up for the person in meetings if they are interrupted or ignored or if you overhear others joking about them or the identity category that describes them.

If you yourself are part of one or more marginalized groups and you find it difficult to be an ally, then form allied groups with others. You can always make a change; sometimes, it just requires you to find more people who have each other's backs.

Organize reverse mentorships

If you want to widen your horizons and learn more about everyday discrimination, try identifying one or more individuals in your organization or your network who are younger than you, in a more junior position than you, or part of a minority group you do not belong to. Enter a reverse mentorship with this person—that is, a situation in which you are the mentee of the younger/underrepresented person, who acts as your mentor and advises you on how you can become a better colleague/manager, based on their unique perspective.

If you are part of one or more minority groups and do not feel as if you have enough privilege to enter such a reverse mentorship, you can propose an organization-wide reverse mentorship program to the management. If you feel comfortable doing so (this is never something you should feel obligated to do), you can even make yourself available as a mentor.

Final thoughts

Final thoughts

I hope that this book has offered insights into what everyday discrimination is, how it manifests, and the damage that it potentially causes to the individual, the working environment, and the organization's performance. In other words, this is the "knowledge" part of the KAB framework that has been brought forth in this book. I also hope that the research I have presented and the stories I have told have gone straight to your heart—that you now feel in your body how important it is to fight everyday discrimination at work. That is the attitude part. Finally, I hope that you will embrace some of the tools and methods presented here so that *you* and your colleagues can change your behavior and start fighting everyday discrimination in your workplace *today*. Thus, I hope to have answered the question invoked in the book's title: *How do we fight everyday discrimination at work?*

One thing is certain—fighting everyday discrimination at work pays off. At the individual level, it increases job satisfaction and well-being by improving psychological safety and fostering inclusion and acknowledgment. Since happy and safe employees perform better, it also pays off at the organizational level—and literally on the bottom line.

To illustrate how workplaces can evolve if we become better at fighting everyday discrimination, let us revisit the four vignettes from the beginning and imagine how they could have turned out if the participants in the stories had actively fought everyday discrimination.

We begin with a large Danish organization in the construction industry. Mehmet is a newly hired apprentice. He has already developed good relationships with his colleagues on the team. One colleague in particular has been looking after him and making sure that he is introduced to all the various aspects of the job. Their interactions are friendly and informal. After his first week, Mehmet has to clock his hours on his time card. The more experienced colleague offers to take care of it for him, and for this, he asks Mehmet for his full name. On hearing the name, the colleague laughs and says, "That is a real terrorist name." Mehmet is shocked by the comment, but he does not even get to react before his other colleague, Thomas, says, "Hey, I don't like it when you connect Mehmet to terrorism like that." The more experienced colleague takes a second to think and then replies, "You're right. That was actually not very funny. I'm sorry, Mehmet. I didn't mean it like that. Are we OK?" Mehmet is relieved. He is very used to hearing jokes about Muslims and terrorism, and he is shaken every time. However, right now, he is feeling both seen and included. He is proud of working at a company where the culture is supportive of people's differences and where there is room for making mistakes and getting the chance to apologize.

The second example takes us to the Danish headquarters of a large international consulting firm. Julie is twenty-seven years old, and she has worked in the organization for a year and a half. She loves her job and working long hours, and she is thriving in the competitive environment of the consulting business. One day, her manager approaches her and says, "Julie, I think you are working too much. The other partners and I have discussed how we can best support our junior consultants. We know that, at your age, a lot of decisions have to be made, and honestly, a lot of us have regrets about the decisions we made. So we have decided to initiate mentorships for all the junior consultants. That way, we can adjust the workload for each and every one of you based on where you are in your lives. I want you to know that I value you a lot, and if you ever want to have children or your life situation changes in any other way, I would like to help you choose the proper tasks that will give you a meaningful working life here and allow you to pursue your career goals—no matter your other life choices." Julie is very surprised and touched by these words. She has heard so many rumors about the "up-or-out" culture in the consulting business, but her manager's words make her feel seen and appreciated. She also feels that she can talk to her manager if she ever needs it. At the same time, she is very excited about the mentorship, and she hopes that it will be able to help her. She has already been feeling the weight of the many difficult choices she is facing, and she is not completely sure about what she wants, but now, knowing that the organization will support her no matter what, she feels a lot safer.

The third example takes us to a Danish university. Peter is teaching a new class of students, and he has been looking forward to getting to know them. As he is developing a relationship with the class, one student, Emilie, starts paying him an unusual amount of attention. Peter notices how Emilie stands very close to him whenever he is talking to a group of students after class. Over time, Emilie's attention intensifies, and she also starts attending his other classes. One day, as Peter is reading one of her papers and checking the references, he finds that one of them contains a direct link to a pornographic website. He is shocked. He decides to confront Emilie and tell her to stop, but Emilie does not understand why he does not like the attention. Her behavior continues. Peter tells his colleagues about the situation. They are all supportive and share his belief that this is not OK. All of them turn to the head of the department, who also takes the situation very seriously. They all agree that they should not confront Emilie directly, seeing as she is also in a precarious situation since Peter is her teacher and has to grade her for the exam. Instead, they plan an intervention for the next class in which they will address ethics and morale by presenting a sequence of vignettes and then discuss with the students what is considered acceptable behavior. One of the vignettes is about displaying pornographic material. The class progresses really well. The students are passionately engaged in the discussion, and in the end, they agree on a code of *conduct*—not only for the classroom but also for the way they want to behave in their future workplaces. After the session, Emilie stops behaving inappropriately with Peter, and for the remaining classes, she acts like the other students. Peter feels seen and acknowledged by his colleagues. He greatly appreciates their strong sense of solidarity, and he is feeling motivated to work more actively with ethics and morale to create an inclusive space in his future classes.

For the fourth and final example, we turn to a Danish public organization. Martin is making his way to the reception to meet a candidate whom he is interviewing for a new position. He has a very good feeling about her, and he is looking forward to meeting her and finding out if she is the right candidate for the job. He greets her politely by shaking her hand and welcoming her, and then they walk toward the meeting room, where the interview will take place. They engage in small talk on the way. Martin asks her what she likes to do in her spare time, and she replies that she loves kayaking with her wife and that they are trying to convince their children to also get into kayaking. Martin is baffled for half a second, but then he remembers his training in following up on open-ended questions and asks how old the children are. By doing so, Martin quickly brings the conversation back to his own comfort zone, but he does so without dismissing the trust the candidate has shown him by being open about her sexual orientation and family life.

In the rewritten (and, unfortunately, fictive) versions of their experiences, Mehmet, Julie, Peter, and Martin have all gone from being in confusing, stressful, and hurtful situations that create frustration and potentially resignations to being in—and helping create—workplaces in which the employees are respected as individuals, resulting in increased well-being at work and strong colleagueship. Moving from a working environment affected by everyday discrimination to an environment characterized by respect and inclusion has positive effects at individual, organizational, and societal levels.

References

Agerström, J. & Rooth, D-O. (2009). Implicit Prejudice and Ethnic Minorities: Arab-Muslims in Sweden. *International Journal of Manpower*, 30, 43–55.

Ahmed, S. (2012). *On Being Included: Racism and Diversity in Institutional Life*. Durham: Duke University Press.

Crenshaw, K. (1989). Demarginalizing the Intersection of Race and Sex: A Black Feminist Critique of Antidiscrimination Doctrine, Feminist Theory and Antiracist Politics. *University of Chicago Legal Forum*, 1989(1), 139–167.

Eckes, T. (2002). Paternalistic and Envious Gender Stereotypes: Testing Predictions From the Stereotype Content Mode. *Sex Roles*, 47, 99–114.

Essed, P. (1991). *Understanding Everyday Racism: An Interdisciplinary Theory*. Thousand Oaks, CA: Sage.

Glick, P. & Fiske, S.T. (1996). The Ambivalent Sexism Inventory: Differentiating Hostile and Benevolent Sexism. *Journal of Personality and Social Psychology*, 70(3), 491–512.

Greenland, K., Andreouli, E., Augoustinos, M., & Taulke-Johnson, R. (2018). What Constitutes 'Discrimination' in Everyday Talk? Argumentative Lines and the Social Representations of Discrimination. *Journal of Language and Social Psychology*, 37(5), 541–561.

Khawaja, I. (2022). Minoritetsstress: Begrebet, Dets Anvendelighed og Potentiale [Minority Stress: The Concept, Its Usability, and Potential]. *Kvinder, Køn og Forskning*, 2, 91–107.

Krøjer, J. et al. (2023). *Sexisme på Arbejde* [Sexism at Work]. København: Djøf Forlag.

Luthra, P. & Muhr, S.L. (2023). *Leading Through Bias: 5 Essential Skills to Block Bias and Improve Inclusion at Work*. London: Palgrave.

Moss-Racusin, C.A., Dovidio, J.F., Brescoll, V.L., Graham, M., & Handelsman, J. (2012). Science Faculty's Subtle Gender Biases Favor Male Students. *PNAS: Proceedings of the National Academy of Sciences for the United States of America*, 109(41), 16474–16479.

Muhr, S.L. (2019). *Ledelse af Køn* [Gendered Leadership]. København: DJØF Forlag.

Skadegård, M.C. & Horst, C. (2021). Between a Rock and a Hard Place: A Study of Everyday Racism, Racial Discrimination, and Racial Microaggressions in Contemporary Denmark. *Social Identities*, 27(1), 92–113.

Williams, J.C. (2021). *Bias Interrupted: Creating Inclusion for Real and for Good*. Brighton, MA: Harvard Business Press.

Endnotes

1. For a more thorough discussion of the terms, see Luthra and Muhr, 2023.

2. All individuals have been anonymized with pseudonyms, and the organizations remain anonymous as well.

3. For a longer version of this story, you can go to www.sexismedu.dk and download the free book Sexism in Danish Higher Education and Research.

4. The term "race" is purposely placed in quotation marks because there is only one human race. "Race" is a social construct in which certain skin colors and physical features have been assigned certain meanings.

5. Let us dwell for a moment on the terms "Western" and "non-Western," considering where "the Western" countries are located. First, note that western is a relative position on a globe that is round, but when we look at most maps, Europe is in the middle. Second, the countries that are consi-

dered "Western" include North America, Europe, Australia, and New Zealand. There is nothing particularly western about the location of these countries, is there? Nevertheless, "Western" and "non-Western" are terms many national registers use as a basis for data analysis—for example, labeling some people as "immigrants from non-Western countries."

6. As this book is written from a Danish perspective, I refer to Danish legislation in this section. Please see Luthra and Muhr (2023) for a more global take or consult the operative rules of your jurisdiction.

7. https://danskelove.dk/forskelsbehandlingsloven

8. https://danskelove.dk/ligebehandlingsloven

9. https://fiu-ligestilling.dk/tools-and-materials/diskrimination-og-usaglig-forskelsbehandling/

10. In this section on "gender," I primarily refer to research that draws on a binary understanding of gender—that is, men versus women. In the section below on sexual orientation and gender identity, I include studies on non-cisgender identities, such as transgender and non-binary identities. This is because discrimination toward men

and women often relies on sexism, whereas discrimination toward transgender and non-binary people is heavily influenced by heterosexism as well.

11. National Monitoring of the Working Environment among Wage Earners, 2021, The Danish Working Environment Authority (Arbejdstilsynet)

12. The National Integration Barometer: https://integrationsbarometer.dk/tal-og-analyser/filer-tal-og- analyser/arkiv/BaggrundstabellerfraMedborgerskabsundersgelsen2020.pdf

13. https://videnskab.dk/kultur-samfund/folkeskolelaerere-diskriminerer-drenge-med-mellemoestlige-navne

14. This is a simplification since Q sometimes is also seen as covering sexual orientation, that is as comprising all those who don't identify as heterosexual or cisgender.

15. https://menneskeret.dk/lgbt-barometer/lgbt-hvad-hvor-mange

16. https://alsresearch.dk/projekt/lgbti-personers-trivsel-paa-arbejdsmarkedet/

17. This is freely downloadable at www.sexismedu.dk, and an updated Danish version is also available (see Krøjer et al., 2023).

18. Poornima Luthra and I present a more elaborate list in our book Leading Through Bias.

19. For more tools and methods, see, for example, the free book Sexism in Higher Education and Research on www.sexismedu.dk or Luthra and Muhr (2023).

20. The book can be downloaded at www.sexismedu.dk. It also comes with a free podcast in which episode 2 focuses on the vignette technique, and in every episode, 2–3 vignettes are read out loud and discussed. The podcast, Do You Know Sexism, can be found here: https://www.spreaker.com/show/do-you-know-sexism.

21. See Luthra (2022) for more tips and ideas on how to become an active ally.

www.ingramcontent.com/pod-product-compliance
Lightning Source LLC
Chambersburg PA
CBHW071943210526
45479CB00002B/793